Knight Book of Fun and Games for a Rainy Day

Gyles Brandreth

Illustrated by David Farris

KNIGHT BOOKS
Hodder & Stoughton

ISBN 0 340 19781 1
Text copyright © 1976 Gyles Brandreth
Illustrations copyright © 1976 Hodder & Stoughton Limited

First published in 1976 by Knight, the paperback division of
Hodder & Stoughton Children's Books, Salisbury Road, Leicester

Printed and bound in Great Britain by
Cox & Wyman Ltd, London, Reading and Fakenham

KNIGHT BOOK OF FUN AND GAMES FOR A RAINY DAY

If you've ever been marooned indoors on a rainy day and not known what to do, here is the book for you. Do you like umbrella games, board games, do-it-yourself home movies or just puzzling brain-teasers and quizzes? This book has lots of ideas.

CONTENTS

Board Games for a Rainy Day   43

String Games for a Rainy Day   69

Puzzles for a Rainy Day   76

Quizzes for a Rainy Day   96

INTRODUCTION

The rain it raineth every day,
Upon the just and unjust fella,
But more upon the just because
The unjust hath the just's umbrella!

That little poem is one of my favourites and whenever I see anyone caught out of doors in the rain without an umbrella I think of it. Of course, what the poet says isn't quite true. The rain it raineth *not* every day. The rain it certainly raineth a great deal, but never anywhere in the world, I'm pleased to say, for three hundred and sixty-five days in the year.

However, in our part of the world there definitely do seem to be a lot of very wet days and this book is designed to help you make the most of them. I've enjoyed writing the book because I'm someone who just loves rainy days. That's to say, I love them when I'm on the inside looking out. I hate them when I'm on the outside looking in. I have never enjoyed standing in the rain – with or without an umbrella – and why people like singing and dancing in the rain (and some do, no doubt about it) I'll never understand.

My idea of the best place to be on a rainy day is indoors and by a warm fire. And my idea of the best things to do on a rainy day you will find in the pages that follow. With a bit of luck you may want to go on doing some of them even when the sky has cleared and the sun is shining. And I'm hoping that the do-it-yourself chess set will last you a lifetime.

I am sorry to say there are two things I wanted very much

to include in the book, but I sadly haven't been able to. The publishers said it would be too difficult to bind them. It's a pity because, in my opinion, a rainy day isn't any fun at all without them. You'll have guessed what I mean by now. Yes: tea and hot buttered toast. Have some right away and by the time you've finished you'll be feeling so good I *know* you'll enjoy the book!

GYLES BRANDRETH

Mishmash for a Rainy Day

Umbrella Maze Number One
[Solution page 122]

WORDS FOR A RAINY DAY

The dictionary says the word *mishmash* means 'an odd and delightful mixture' – which is just what this first chapter hopes to be. To get it going, can you begin by thinking of the different words that would fit these dictionary definitions?

1 'Condensed moisture of atmosphere falling visibly in separate drops.'
2 'Light circular canopy of material attached to radiating folding frame sliding on stick carried in the hand.'
3 'Arch showing prismatic colours in their order formed in the sky.'
4 'Visible electric discharge between clouds or cloud and ground.'
5 'A coat or cloak made of a waterproof material of rubber and cloth.'
6 'Mass of visible condensed watery vapour floating high above the general level of the ground.'
7 'A waterproof hat with a broad rim behind to protect the neck.'
8 'Pellets of frozen vapour that fall in a shower.'
9 'Overshoes made of rubber designed to keep shoes clean or dry.'
10 'Air in more or less natural motion, being either a breeze or a gale or a blast.'

(Answers on page 41)

RECORDING THE RAINFALL

Well, if it *is* going to rain you might as well make the most of it and record the rainfall. It's not difficult to do: just place a clean, empty jam jar somewhere out of doors and every so often measure the amount of rain you've collected. Check to see how much rainwater is in the jar each morning and night and make a chart showing how much rain falls every day.

People often think of Great Britain as a very rainy country, but in fact it's drier than most. In England and Wales we can expect between 25 and 35 inches of rainfall in a year and in Scotland between 45 and 55 inches, which sounds quite a lot, but is rather modest when you compare it with the world's wettest area, Cherrapunji in Assam, where they expect to get 400 inches of rainfall every year.

As you can see from the list on the next page, which represents the average rainfall in different parts of Great Britain in recent years, the amount of rain you are likely to get depends on where you live. On the whole, it's wetter in Glasgow than it is in Nottingham and drier in Oxford than in most places.

What will probably surprise you – and perhaps disappoint you – is to find how little water there seems to be in your jam jar every time you go to check it. On 18th July, 1964, at Preston in Lancashire a total of 2.21 inches of rain fell in only five minutes, and on 14th August, 1975, in North London there was a deluge of 6.72 inches of rain, but those are records, so every time you look into *your* jar you can expect to find a lot, lot less.

In Britain, Australia, New Zealand, Canada and America, the

rainfall is still recorded in inches. If you want to be ahead of times, you can always record your rainfall in centimetres. Here is a list of British towns with the average annual rainfall recorded in those towns in recent years. See how it compares with the rainfall where you live.

Aberystwyth	34 inches
Balmoral	27
Bath	21
Birmingham	22
Bournemouth	24
Cambridge	18
Cardiff	33
Douglas	38
Dumfries	39
Durham	20
Eastbourne	30
Edinburgh	20
Glasgow	36
Huddersfield	29
Hull	18
Lincoln	16
Liverpool	22
London	21
Manchester	28
Margate	18
Nottingham	17
Oxford	16
Scarborough	16
Sheffield	25
Skegness	18
Southampton	24
Torquay	26
Weymouth	21

TWINKLE-TOES

This is a fun thing to do on a rainy day if you happen to have a pair of old plain plimsolls and your mother doesn't mind what you do with them. The idea is simply this: with a felt-tip coloured marker you decorate the shoes. You cover them with flowers or funny faces or pretty patterns – and then, of course, you wear them.

(Remember that the ink in the coloured markers is usually permanent, so draw your patterns and pictures with care because once you have decorated the shoes you can't undecorate them!)

PAPER PLATE MASKS

To go with your multi-coloured plimsolls, make a multi-coloured mask. Get hold of a large, plain paper plate and paint a funny face on to it. If you want to be able to see where you are going, cut out holes for the eyes and if you want to be able to breath make a hole for the nose. Punch a small hole on either side of the plate (at about ear level) and tie a piece of string or elastic through the two holes so as to be able to keep the mask on.

DO-IT-YOURSELF CARTOON

On the outside corners of the pages of an old book or an old magazine draw a series of small pictures and make each picture change slightly, so that as you flick through the pages with your thumb the pictures will seem to move and you will find you have created an animated cartoon. This is how Walt Disney started, so before you know where you are you'll probably discover you've invented a new Mickey Mouse.

DO-IT-YOURSELF JUMBLE SALE

Now here's a marvellous idea for earning some extra pocket money or raising funds for a favourite charity: put on your own jumble sale and invite all your friends to come and buy. You can set up your stall in your bedroom or the hall or, better still, in the garage if you have one. You will only want to charge a few pence for the items you have got to sell, but the more things you have on display the more people will enjoy the sale. Try making most of the produce yourself – home-made biscuits, home-made cakes, sweets, jellies, glasses of lemonade – and collect the other items from around the house – old toys, old books, old magazines, old games – but be sure you don't sell anything that doesn't belong to you or anything your family thinks you should keep.

Of course, if it really *is* a very rainy day you can always try selling fresh rainwater at twopence a jar!

DO-IT-YOURSELF BEAUTY SALON

Why not set up and run your own beauty salon? All you need is a dressing table, a chair, a brush, a comb, a selection of cosmetics, a nail file and an emery board. With the brush and comb you can create fashionable hair styles; with the make-up you can decorate faces in all sorts of ways; and with the nail file and emery board you can give manicures.

When you have set up shop invite your friends round for a free visit to the beautician.

HOME MOVIES

Here's a way to create your own films at home. Get hold of a cheap roll of toilet paper and on each sheet draw a different picture. As you draw the pictures you will have to unwind the roll carefully so that the paper won't tear. When you have drawn all the pictures you need to invent the story you are going to tell and roll up the toilet paper again. Now you can show your film. When the audience is ready all you have to do is unroll the roll, tell your story and wait for the applause.

OMELETTE

What are the eggs that are so superb? Why, *excellent*, of course! What are the eggs that keep you fit? Why, *exercise*, to be sure! What are the eggs that are so precise? Why, *exact*, naturally!

The idea is simple: we are looking for words that begin with *ex* but we're pronouncing *ex* as *eggs*. Can you help?

1 What are the eggs that magnify things?
2 What are the eggs you have to take at school?
3 What are the eggs that set you a pattern to follow?
4 What are the eggs that involve give and take?
5 What are the eggs that make you cry out?
6 What are the eggs that go an outing?
7 What are the eggs that lose you your head?
8 What are the eggs that leave you completely tired out?
9 What are the eggs you put on display?
10 What are the eggs that make you grow?
11 What are the eggs that show you the way out?
12 What are the eggs to which you look forward?
13 What are the eggs that set you off on a journey?
14 What are the eggs that cost a lot?
15 What are the eggs that are quite remarkable?

(Answers on page 41)

DO-IT-YOURSELF PACK OF CARDS

Playing cards are getting more and more expensive to buy, so why don't you take advantage of the rainy day and make yourself a pack of your own? You must begin by cutting up fifty-two pieces of card. These cards can be any size and any shape, as long as all 52 are the same size and shape. The standard size for a playing card is about 10cms by 5cms. When you have made the cards you mark them up, so that you end up with four sets with thirteen cards in each set – an Ace, 2, 3, 4, 5, 6, 7, 8, 9, 10, Jack, Queen and King. Traditionally the four sets are made up with hearts, diamonds, spades and clubs, but you can choose your own symbols: apples, oranges, pears and bananas, for example, or cars, trains, planes and boats, or dogs, cats, cows and pigs. When all the cards have been marked on one side, you must decorate the reverse side of each card. You can choose any pattern you like, but the pattern should be the same for each card on this side.

When the pack is complete, celebrate with a game of Snap.

PICTURE MESSAGES

See how many messages you can write using pictures and symbols instead of words. It sounds easier than it is, but to give you an idea here are a couple of examples:

WHY ARE YOU SAD?

I LOVE YOU

JUMBLED WEATHER FORECAST

Here is a weather forecast for the whole of the United Kingdom where the unfortunate weather forecaster seems to have got some of the most important words jumbled. Can you unjumble the words and make sense of the forecast?

Here is the weather forecast for the whole of the United Kingdom for the next twenty-four hours. In southern England the NAIR will continue, with the possibility of LIAH tonight in some parts. In the Midlands and the North severe MORTSS are likely, with violent URHDTEN and GGIITHNLN throughout the evening. In Scotland WONS is forecast this afternoon, with GOF this evening which will mean poor IIIISBYTLV on all roads, so drive with care. Northern Ireland can also expect MYROST weather, with IRAN turning to LEEST. There will be CIY SCHETAP on most roads. The only part of the United Kingdom where we can expect the weather to be at all RAIF is the Isle of Wight, where there is a possibility that the DOLCUS will clear this afternoon and there may even be a few hours of INNEHUSS. All in all the situation is TAINNUCER and the outlook LEAKB.

(Answers on page 42)

BALLOON FACES

You can play all sorts of splendid indoor games with balloons – one of the best is the one where you and a friend toss the balloon between you, and whoever lets it touch the ground first is the loser – but every single one of them is so much more enjoyable if it is played with beautifully decorated balloons. The way to decorate a blown-up balloon is simply to hold it firmly to you with one hand and draw on it very gently with the other using a felt tip marker. If you haven't yet blown up the balloon you can draw on it before you blow it up, always remembering, of course, that when you blow it up the size of whatever you have drawn will greatly expand.

Of course, you don't only have to paint faces on the balloons. You can paint on pretty patterns and messages as well.

COMIC COLOURING

Collect together your favourite newspaper cartoon strips and spend some time colouring in the drawings. If you have a friend, each of you can colour a different cartoon strip and when you have finished you can find a grown-up or another friend who can judge the pictures and tell you which one they think is best.

IF I HAD £1,000,000

If you had a million pounds, how would you spend it? Would you spend it all on sweets or sports cars or holidays in the sun? Would you give it away and if you did, who would you give it to? There's no more entertaining way of spending a wet afternoon than by working out how you would spend £1,000,000.

Here's one list of ideas:

One small castle in Scotland	£ 145,000.00
One small aeroplane	£ 62,000.00
One Rolls Royce motor car	£ 23,000.00
One motor-bike	£ 500.00
One gold-plated pogo stick	£ 100.00
Luxury holiday in Australia	£ 2,400.00
Ocean racing yacht	£ 170,000.00
Presents to parents	£ 200,000.00
£100,000 to each of three brothers and sisters	£ 300,000.00
Supply of ice cream for life	£ 2,000.00
Large stable and 20 ponies	£ 45,000.00
Indoor heated swimming pool	£ 5,000.00
Supply of roast beef and Yorkshire pudding for life	£ 10,000.00
Private football pitch	£ 34,000.00
Grand banquet for 100 guests	£ 900.00
Pedigree pussy cat	£ 95.00
De Luxe Scrabble set	£ 5.00
	£1,000,000.00

Now how would you spend *your* million?

DO-IT-YOURSELF TV

Find yourself a large sheet of brown wrapping paper. It needs to be at least 1 metre square. On to the paper draw the front of a television set, with a large screen, on-off switch and volume and picture controls. Cut out the screen and throw it away. Now hang the sheet over the side of a table, sticking it to the table with sticky tape at the top. Sit under the table with your face showing through the screen. You're all set to make your own television programmes.

ALPHABET PICTURE

Go through some old magazines until you come across a large picture containing lots of different things. Now take a pair of scissors and cut out an object from the picture beginning with the letter A, then cut out an object beginning with the letter B, then C, then D, and so on, going on through the alphabet as far as you can.

If you have got a friend with you, give him another picture and get him to start cutting out objects at the same time as you do. The first player to have cut out 26 objects is the winner. At the end of a set time limit the player who has cut out most objects is the winner.

PASTA PICTURES

Collect together a good selection of pieces of uncooked pasta – spaghetti, noodles, macaroni and all. Now break up the pasta and use the bits to make up a picture. Glue the pieces to some card and you'll have created a picture that's so good you could almost eat it!

SOAP SCULPTURE

This is great fun, but don't do it until you've been given permission! Get yourself a large bar of soap and with a bluntish knife or a potato peeler, carve the soap. You can either draw patterns on to the soap or, better still, actually sculpt it into a particular shape.

CAT'S CASTLE

If you happen to have a cat you'll know that they love playing in boxes. Why not turn a box – an old shoe box or a large food carton will do – into a cat's castle? All you have to do is paint the outside of the box with doors and windows and turrets and hand it over to the cat. It won't take him long to make it home.

BUBBLE BATH

When it's raining outside and the wind is blowing, there's nothing nicer than a lovely hot bath. And to make the bath twice as much fun, you can colour the water and fill it with bubbles.

To colour the water pour in six tiny drops of food colouring (no more) as you begin to let the taps run. To make the bubbles squirt a little washing-up liquid under the running water. A little goes a long, long way, so don't overdo it or you'll find you have filled the whole bathroom with bubbles before you know where you are.

BUBBLE BLOW

If you don't feel like having a bath, but *do* feel like blowing some bubbles, you can always blow your own. Make a mixture of warm water, soap flakes and a little cooking oil. Dip an ordinary drinking straw into the mixture and blow gently. Because of the oil, the bubbles you blow will last longer. See how many you can make and keep afloat at a time.

SQUIGGLE SCRIBBLE

This is a game to play with a friend and you will need pencils and paper before you start. To begin, one of the players draws a squiggle on a piece of paper, like this:

He passes the squiggle to the other player who has to turn the squiggle into a recognisable picture, like this:

When a player manages to turn a squiggle into a proper picture he scores a point. If he can't make anything out of the squiggle he scores nothing. Players take it in turns to draw the squiggle and at the end of a set number of rounds the player with the highest score is the winner.

SO YOU THINK YOU CAN SPELL?

If you think you can spell, here's a challenge for you. In this list of twenty words, five are wrongly spelt. Which five?

1 Apostle
2 Caterpilar
3 Rythm
4 Mathematics
5 Interpretation
6 Antedeluvian
7 Shamrock
8 Avocado
9 Scolarship
10 Cosmetics
11 Caricature
12 Antelope
13 Punctual
14 Amphitheatre
15 Rhubarb
16 Restarant
17 Calories
18 Rhododendron
19 Extravegent
20 Indivisibility

(Answers on page 42)

MIRROR, MIRROR ON THE WALL

It's in the story of *Snow White and the Seven Dwarfs* that the wicked queen is forever asking:

> Mirror, mirror on the wall,
> Who is the fairest one of all?

The answer, of course, is always Snow White. However, if you don't happen to have a very talkative mirror in your home, don't despair. Even a silent mirror can provide a lot of fun. Ask your mother or your grandmother (or a sister, cousin or aunt) if you can have some old lipstick and then get to work drawing pictures on the mirror!

When you have finished, be sure to give the mirror a thorough clean.

MORE MAKE-UP

If your mother *will* lend you some old lipstick, but *won't* let you make any marks on the mirror, ask her if you can make yourself up instead. Borrow all the make-up she will let you use (and get hold of old stage make-up as well, if you can) and set to work sitting in front of the mirror. You can turn yourself into a clown or a red indian or simply decorate your face as you like.

If you have a friend, why not take it in turns to make each other up?

DOUGH FOR FUN'S SAKE

If you have ever been to see a Christmas pantomime, the chances are that you will remember a scene in the kitchen where two characters are trying to make a cake, but spend most of the time throwing dough at each other. Well, dough is easy to make and great fun to play with, but unless you want to get into a lot of trouble at home don't start throwing it around the house!

Begin by putting on an apron and getting together all the ingredients. You will need two cups of flour, half a cup of salt and a quarter of a cup of warm water. Add the salt to the warm water and stir it until the salt completely dissolves. Add this mixture to the flour and knead it all thoroughly until you have made your dough. Now shape the dough as you please.

DOUGH FOR ART'S SAKE

You can make another kind of dough that will harden like clay and it's a good idea to do this if you plan to make any dough sculptures that you think you might like to keep. Begin by mixing together two cups of flour with one cup of salt, now add just enough water to make a very stiff dough. (You can also add food colouring if you want to create coloured sculptures). Shape the dough as you want it and leave it to harden and dry.

UMBRELLA GAME

Here's a game for a rainy day that you can only play if you live in a block of flats where there is a landing where it's safe for you to play or if your house has a big garage attached to it. To play the game you need as many umbrellas as there are players and you must begin by opening the umbrellas and putting them on the ground, so that you are holding the umbrella handle which is facing upwards and the point on top of the umbrella is touching the ground. On the command 'Go!' the players all spin their umbrellas and let go. The winner is the player whose umbrella stays spinning longest.

If you don't mind getting splashed, you will find this is a very good game to play if you have lots of wet umbrellas and you want to dry them quickly.

QUICK SPELL

On sixty-two small pieces of card write down different letters of the alphabet. Put the five vowels, A, E, I, O and U, on four cards each and put the remaining letters on two cards each. When you have made the cards, shuffle them and deal ten of them face downwards to each player. You must now see how many words you can make with the ten letters you have. After three minutes the player who has written down the most words scores a point. After ten rounds, the player with the highest score is the winner.

BALANCING ACT

Get an empty milk bottle and put it on the table in front of you. Now get a box of matches and one by one try to balance as many matches as you can on top of the milk bottle. Every time a match falls off or into the bottle, you must start all over again. When there are as many matches on the bottle as you dare place there, count the number and give the bottle and the matches to a friend to see if he or she can beat your record.

UMBRELLA TOSS

Here's another umbrella game that you can play indoors on a rainy day if you can find an umbrella that isn't being used. All you do is open it up and stand it with its handle in the air. The players stand about 5 metres away from the umbrella and take it in turns to bounce a ping-pong ball into it. Every time a player throws his ping-pong ball and gets it to stay in the umbrella with it bouncing once and only once on its way there, he scores a point. After each player has had ten throws, the player with the highest score is the winner.

THINK OF A NUMBER

Get a friend and explain to him that you have developed special mind-reading powers and that you would like to show these to him. When he agrees, simply say to him: 'Think of a number. Multiply it by three. Add one. Multiply the result by three. And add the total to the number you first thought of. Now give the final total.'

When he tells you the total, you will find that it always ends with a 3. Strike off that three and you will have found the number he first thought of.

Here's an example:

Think of a number, say 4
Multiply it by three 12
Add one 13
Multiply the result by three 39
Add the number you first thought of 43

When you strike off the 3, you are left with 4 and that, of course, is the number first thought of.

And here's another:

Think of a number, say 17
Multiply it by three 51
Add one 52
Multiply the result by three 156
Add the number you first thought of 173

Yet again, when you strike off the 3, you find you are left with the original number, in this case 17.

And here, just to prove it works even when you get up into the millions, is one last example:

Think of a number, say	9,284,716
Multiply it by three	27,854,148
Add one	27,854,149
Multiply the result by three	83,562,447
Add the number you first thought of	92,847,163

And of course, once you have taken away the final 3, you find you are left with the original 9,284,716.

THE MAP RACE

This is a game for two players and to play it you need two identical maps of the same city. The more detailed the maps are the better the game will be. All you do is give one map to each player and on the word 'Go!' give them both the name of a street. The first player to find that street on the map gains a point. After ten rounds, the player with most points is the winner.

TIME CHECK

A very useful thing to do on a wet day when time seems to drag is to see that all the watches and clocks are telling exactly the right time. Begin by checking the time yourself, listening for it on the radio or by dialling the correct telephone number for the 'Speaking Clock' which will give you the exact time every ten seconds. When you know the precise time, adjust your own watch, then go round the house checking on all the other clocks and watches.

STORAGE JARS

Do you happen to have collections of any of the odd items on this list?

Pens and pencils
Stamps
Coins
Pebbles
Shells
Feathers
Matchboxes
Toy soldiers
Dolls' clothes
Paper clips and drawing pins
Marbles
Packs of playing cards

If you do and you don't happen to have anywhere to store them, here's an idea you could find useful. See if you can find a large, empty jar with a screw-on lid – one pound jars for instant coffee are the kind to look out for. When you've found the jar, clean it thoroughly inside, wash off the label and stick on your own label. Then fill the jar with all your own odds and ends.

HOLLOW BOOK

Another good idea for a special place to store things is inside
a book. Get hold of an old book that nobody has any more
use for and cut out a square in the centre of each page so
that you have built a hollow compartment inside the book.
It's the perfect hiding place for anything you want to keep
secretly.

INK AUTOGRAPHS

In Victorian days this was a very popular thing to do. Take
an ordinary piece of writing paper and fold it in half. Now
unfold it and, in ink (or with paint), write your name along
the fold. Before the ink has time to dry, fold the piece of
paper again and press it firmly. After a moment, unfold it
once more and you will find you have created an interesting
pattern. The Victorians used to think that the pattern
represented the shape you would have when one day you
became a ghost!

HOW TO GET TO SLEEP IN A STORM

If you are lying awake in a thunderstorm and simply can't get to sleep, start counting the thunderclaps. Before you have counted twenty, you will find you have dozed off. If that doesn't work, close your eyes and imagine the rain sleeting down. Try counting the raindrops as they pass in front of your eyes.

INDOOR CAMP

In many ways, camping at home is even more fun than camping out of doors. For one thing, you won't get wet. And for another, you'll be much more comfortable. Plan your indoor camping expedition just as you would plan an outdoor one. Pack a sleeping bag and a tent and plenty to eat and drink. When you set out, instead of disappearing into the woods, you disappear into your bedroom, where you set up your tent, lay out your sleeping bag, eat your picnic and settle down for a good night's rest.

CROSSWORD FOR A RAINY DAY

Clues Across

1 In the song, these keep falling on your head.
5 It isn't a rose, but it *is* the name of a flower and the name of a girl.
6 If ever you help a criminal you will be taken to court because it is a crime to aid and to —.
7 We call it a lift. What do the Americans call it?
9 Judy Garland sang about one of these when she played the part of Dorothy in the film of *The Wizard of Oz*.

Clues Down

1 Santa Claus would be lost without them.
2 It's pointed and sharp and made of frozen water.
3 Beatrix Potter invented one called Peter and another called Benjamin.
4 These are lovely fields for sheep and cows to graze in.
8 A very small lorry.

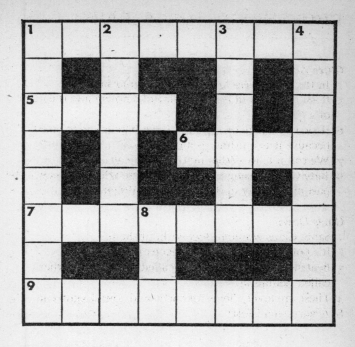

(Answers on page 42)

JOKES FOR A RAINY DAY

Ask a silly question
'What's the weather like outside?'
'Don't ask me. It's so cloudy I can't see.'

Wrong job
There was once a very famous weatherman on television
who always got the forecast wrong. Eventually the BBC
decided they would have to sack the man, so they wrote to
him and asked him to look for another job. The letter ended,
'We think too that you might like to look for a job abroad,
because obviously over here the climate doesn't agree with
you.'

The meeting of two minds
    Street beggar to grand lady: I've seen better days, madam–
    Grand lady to street beggar: And so have I, my man, but
                       I haven't the time now to
                       discuss the weather with
                       complete strangers.

Lone Brolly
'Hello, old man, I wonder if you could let me have back that
umbrella I lent you last week.'
'Actually, it's a bit awkward. You see, I've lent it to a friend
of mine. Do you need it badly?'
'Well, not really. It's just that the fellow I borrowed it from
says the owner wants it.'

MISHMASH ANSWERS

WORDS FOR A RAINY DAY

1 Rain
2 Umbrella
3 Rainbow
4 Lightning
5 Macintosh (Note how you spell it! It's Macintosh not Mackintosh because it's named after Mr C. Macintosh who invented it. He died in 1843.)
6 Clouds
7 Sou'wester
8 Hail
9 Galoshes
10 Wind

OMELETTE

1 Exaggerate
2 Examination
3 Example
4 Exchange
5 Exclaim
6 Excursion
7 Execution
8 Exhausted
9 Exhibition
10 Expand
11 Exit
12 Expect
13 Expedition
14 Expensive
15 Extraordinary

JUMBLED WEATHER FORECAST

RAIN, HAIL, STORMS, THUNDER, LIGHTNING, SNOW,
FOG, VISIBILITY, STORMY, RAIN, SLEET, ICY PATCHES,
FAIR, CLOUDS, SUNSHINE, UNCERTAIN, BLEAK.

SO YOU THINK YOU CAN SPELL

Caterpillar
Rhythm
Scholarship
Restaurant
Extravagant

CROSSWORD FOR A RAINY DAY

Across
1 Raindrop
5 Iris
6 Abet
7 Elevator
9 Rainbows

Down
1 Reindeer
2 Icicle
3 Rabbit
4 Pastures
8 Van

Board Games for a Rainy Day

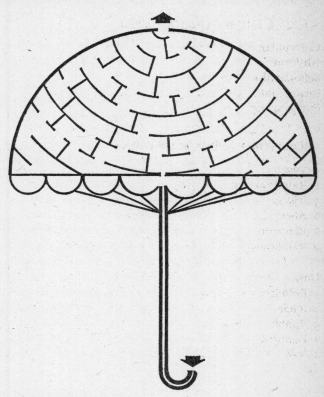

Umbrella Maze Number Two
[Solution on page 123]

CHESS

'Chess is the nourishment of the mind, the solace of the spirit, the brightener of the understanding; wherefore it has been justly preferred by the philosopher, its inventor, to all other means by which we arrive at wisdom.' So said a very flowery Arab called Ali Suli over a thousand years ago. He was exaggerating, of course, but all the same chess *is* a very good game and if you don't know how to play it, a rainy day is the right time to learn.

Millions of people of all ages, from five to ninety-five, play chess and they have been playing the game for thousands of years. It is a game that is easy to learn, but difficult to master. In this chapter we can't hope to do more than introduce you to the game and provide you with your own portable chess set.

Basically, chess is a game for two people and the aim of the game is 'to checkmate your opponent's king'. But, of course, there is much, much more to it than that. How much more you will begin to discover as you play, and the only way to learn how to play well is to play a lot. The more you practise the more skilled you will become, and if you enjoy the game you will want to read some of the hundreds of books that have been written about it. Probably you will also want to join a chess club. There are more than a thousand clubs affiliated to the British Chess Federation and there is almost bound to be one in your area which you can join.

For the time being, here is a brief introduction to one of the world's oldest and most fascinating games.

THE CHESS BOARD

Chess is played on a board of sixty-four squares, alternately black and white. The players sit on either side of the board and each player has a white square at his right-hand lower corner. There are sixteen white pieces for one player and sixteen black pieces for the other player. The pieces are called 'men' and only one 'man' can stand on any one square at a time.

The horizontal rows on the chess board are called ranks and the vertical rows are called files. At the beginning of the game the black men are arranged along the two ranks nearest their player and the white men are arranged along the two ranks nearest their player. From left to right, the back rank of white men is made up like this: a rook, a knight, a bishop, the queen, the king, a bishop, a knight, a rook. The black men run in the same order from right to left. (In this way the white queen will always be on a white square and the black queen on a black square). The second rank on both sides is made up of pawns.

CHESS TERMS

Once you have started to play chess you will want to learn more about the game, but you will probably be annoyed to find that all the books on the subject and all the articles in the papers by the chess correspondents seem to be written in a complicated code. Well, it's not so much a code as a kind of shorthand and it can be quite easily explained.

Each square on the chess board is named after the piece which occupies the square at the head of its file at the beginning of the game. So the square on which the king stands is called K sq., and the squares in the file that stretch directly from it are numbered from 1 to 8. In the same way the square on which the queen stands is called the Q sq., and the squares in the file that stretch from it are also numbered from 1 to 8. The men on the king's side of the board on the back row are called the king's pieces and the pieces on the queen's side of the board are the queen's pieces, so you have the king's bishop (KB) and the queen's bishop (QB) and the king's rook (KR) and the queen's rook (QR) and so on. The board is numbered both from white's and from black's point of view, so, for example, the white queen's bishop's square (white's QB1) is also black's QB8.

In this special shorthand that you will get to know as your interest in the game grows, X means 'takes', ch. stands for 'checks', dis. ch. stands for 'discovered check', o-o signifies 'castles on the king's side', o-o-o signifies 'castles on the queen's side' and e.p. stands for *en passant*, which is French for 'in passing'.

DO-IT-YOURSELF CHESS SET

Before getting down to what the chess terms mean and what the different chess men can and cannot do, let's begin by making a chess set. You can buy a gold-plated chess set for £1,000, but we're giving you this one for nothing. Of course, it won't last as long, but the games of chess you play with it will be just as enjoyable.

Making the Chess Board
To make the chess board, begin by finding a piece of solid cardboard and cutting it so that it is 16 cms square. Then carefully cut out the board pattern that you will find printed on the next two pages and glue it on to the cardboard. (You can always trace this on to some thin card if you don't want to cut the book.) Your chess board is now ready.

Making the Chess Men
You will find the black chess men on pages 51 and 53 and the white chess men on pages 55 and 57. To make the men all you have to do is cut (or trace) around each shape carefully, fold the paper round so that the piece is shaped like a cone and stick it together on the inside with a small piece of Sellotape. Place the men on the right squares and you are ready to play.

The black men

1 A black bishop
   (B for short)

2 A black bishop
   (B for short)

3 The black queen
   (Q for short)

4 The black king
   (K for short)

5 A black rook
   (R for short)

6 A black rook
   (R for short)

The rooks can also be called castles, but the term rook is both more usual and more correct.

7 A black knight
   (Kt for short)

8 A black knight
   (Kt for short)

1
2

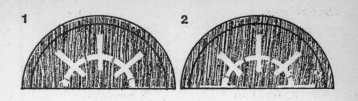

3
4

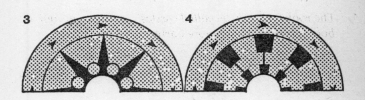

5
6

7
8

The eight black pawns
(all P for short)

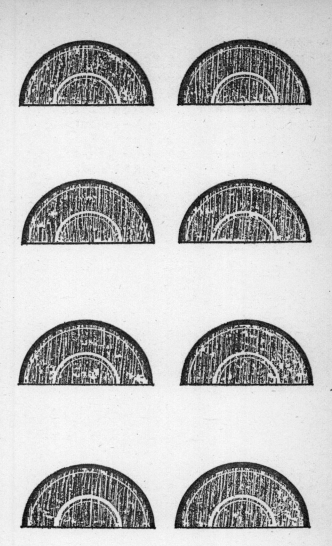

The white men

1 A white bishop
(B for short)

2 A white bishop
(B for short)

3 The white queen
(Q for short)

4 The white king
(K for short)

5 A white rook
(R for short)

6 A white rook
(R for short)

7 A white knight
(Kt for short)

8 A white knight
(Kt for short)

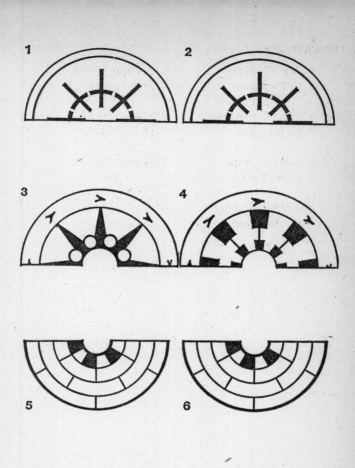

The eight white pawns
(all P for short)

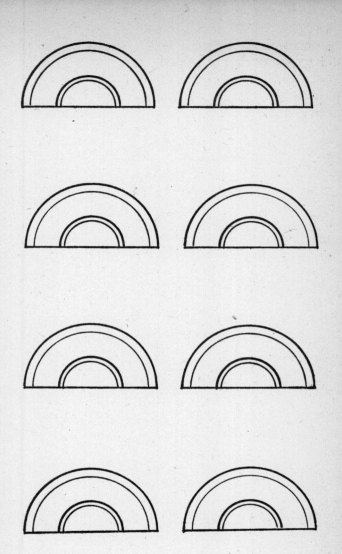

THE GAME

The player with the white men always starts. To decide who will play with the white pieces, one of the players hides a black pawn in one fist and a white pawn in the other. He holds out his fists to his opponent who has to choose the one he wants. The colour of the pawn inside the chosen fist determines the colour of the pieces with which the opponent will play.

The players move alternately and each man can capture one of the enemy's men simply by occupying the square on which the enemy's man was standing. The only man that cannot be captured is the king, but when the king is threatened with being captured he is in 'check' and he must be rescued from this check position before his player can make any other move. When the king cannot escape from a check position the situation is known as 'checkmate' and the king's player has lost the game.

THE MEN AND THEIR MOVES

In a move:

The *rooks* can move any distance along the ranks or the files until their path is blocked. Under no circumstances can they move along diagonals.

The *bishops* can move any distance along diagonals until their path is blocked. Under no circumstances can they move along ranks or files.

The *queen* can move any distance in a straight line along ranks, files or diagonals until she is blocked.

The *king* can move one square in any direction. However, he is not allowed to move himself into a check position.

The *knights* must move in an L-shape, two squares along a rank or a file and then to an adjoining square, either right or left. In making their moves the knights can jump over other chess pieces. They are the only men who are allowed to hop over other pieces like this. (The only other hopping that is allowed in the game comes with *castling*, which is explained later on). All these pieces can move backwards and forwards.

The *pawns* are only allowed to move forward and they must move along their files, except when they are capturing enemy pieces when they have to move one square forward on a diagonal. Pawns may move two squares on their first move, but only one square on each subsequent move. If a pawn moves two squares on its first move and in doing so passes an enemy pawn that would have been able to capture it had it moved one square, the pawn can be captured by the enemy *en passant* on the next move. When a pawn reaches the eighth rank it is 'promoted' and must be replaced on the board by a queen, rook, bishop or knight.

CAPTURING

All the pieces except the pawns capture in the same way. If an enemy piece stands on a square that a king, queen, rook, bishop or knight can move to, the move captures it. The captured enemy piece is then taken off the board and the square it occupied is taken by the piece that captured it.

Pawns capture rather differently. They cannot capture enemy pieces immediately in front of them. They can only capture pieces that are diagonally one square ahead.

CASTLING

Castling is a move that a player can make only once in a game. It involves moving two pieces at once: the king and one rook. The move is only allowed if both pieces are standing in their original positions and neither has already been moved, if the two or the three squares between the king and the rook are empty, if the king is not in check and if the two squares the king must cross are not guarded by the enemy. Castling consists of moving the king two squares towards the rook and then placing the rook on the square just jumped over by the king.

Usually the aim of castling is either to move the king into a more secure position behind unmoved pawns or to bring the rooks closer together towards the centre of the board so that they are in position for a dramatic forward attack.

QUEENING

When a pawn reaches the far side of the board, it must be removed and it can be replaced by a queen or a rook or a bishop or a knight. The usual choice is a queen because it is the most flexible and powerful piece on the board, which, of course, is why the move is known as 'queening'. It is quite legal to replace a pawn with a queen (when the pawn becomes a queen) even if the player still has his original queen on the board. Games with more than two queens on the board are very rare indeed, but it is quite possible and there have been games with as many as five queens on the board at the same time.

MISTAKEN MOVES

At the beginning of the game if any of the pieces have been placed in the wrong position, they can be put back into right position before four moves have been made.

If a man has been touched by a player, the player must then move that man. If he is unable to move that particular man, he must move the king instead, but he cannot move the king by castling. Once a man has been moved and set down, the move is over and second thoughts are not allowed.

WINNING AND LOSING

The aim of the game is to be in a position to capture the enemy king. When a king is in a position to be captured he is in check and if he is unable to move to escape from the check position he has been checkmated and the game is over.

When a player is in a position to capture the enemy king he warns his opponent by saying 'Check!' He isn't obliged to say it, but it is usual. And when a player is in a position to capture the enemy king and the enemy king has no means of escape the player announces his victory by saying 'Checkmate!'

If a player isn't warned that he is in a check position and doesn't notice it himself and makes a move that does not avert the attack, he must simply take his move all over again and do what he can to get himself out of the check position.

Many games don't end with a checkmate, simply because one of the two players resigns because he is sure that his opponent is in a much stronger position and will eventually win. Many other games end in draws.

DRAWN GAMES

A game of chess can end in a draw for half a dozen different reasons and here they are:

Lack of force. This is when the pieces on the board are too weak to force a checkmate on either side.

Perpetual check. This is when one player can show that he can go on and on and on checking the enemy king, without ever being able to checkmate it.

Stalemate. This is when the player whose turn it is to move can make no legal move, but his king is not in check.

Repetition. This is when the same positions of all the pieces, both white and black, occur three times in the same game, with the same player being about to move each time. When this happens for the third time, the player whose turn it is can claim a draw.

The fifty moves rule. Either of the players can claim a draw if during fifty moves by one of the players no pawn has been moved and no pieces have been captured – unless the opponent can demonstrate that he could definitely win.

By agreement. If they want to, the players can agree to a draw. In a tournament game, they are not allowed to do this before the thirtieth turn.

STRATEGY

You could fill a large library with all the books that have been written about chess. Your own local library will probably have a shelf or two. If you want to know more about the different kinds of strategy used by skilled chess players you will have no difficulty finding a book on the subject. There is no room here to go into any of the finer points of the game, but if you need any words of advice to set you on the right path here are some invaluable hints from a remarkable American called Benjamin Franklin. He lived from 1706 to 1790 and was one of the men who helped write the American Declaration of Independence. He was a printer, an author, a statesman, a very wise and witty man and a thoroughly good chess player. According to Benjamin Franklin, the chess player needs three special qualities:

'First, foresight, which looks a little into futurity, and considers the consequences which may attend an action. . . . "If I move this piece, what will be the advantage of my new situation? What use can my adversary make of it to annoy me? What other moves can I make to support it and to defend myself from his attack?"

'Second, the circumspection which surveys the whole chess board, or scene of action, and the relation of the several pieces, and considers the dangers they are respectively exposed to, the several possibilities of aiding each other, the probability that the adversary may take this or that move, and take this or the other piece, and what different means can be used to avoid his stroke, or turns its consequences against him.

'Third, caution not to make our moves too hastily. This habit is best acquired by observing strictly the laws of the game, such as, if you touch a piece you must move it somewhere; if you set it down you just let it stand; and it is therefore best that these rules be observed, as the game thereby becomes so much the more like human life, and particularly of war, in which, if you have incautiously put yourself into a bad or dangerous position you cannot obtain your enemy's leave to withdraw your troops and place them with more security, but must abide the consequences of your folly.'

DRAUGHTS

Now that you have got your own chess board, you will be interested to learn that you can use it for several other games apart from chess, the best known one, of course, being draughts. Draughts is another ancient game about which countless books have been written, but its rules are simpler to explain than those of chess.

To play the game you need one board, two players and twenty-four counters. Traditionally the counters are small, flat circular slices of wood, twelve white and twelve black, but, if you want, you can play the game with a dozen buttons and a dozen shells or with a dozen pennies and a dozen milk bottle tops.

As in chess, the players sit on either side of the board, and each player has a white square at his right-hand lower corner, but, unlike chess, it is the player with the black pieces who always makes the first move. Again the game differs from chess in that the pieces are all placed on the black squares and can only move from one black square to another. Each player places his twelve counters on the black squares on the first three rows facing him.

Because the game is played only on the black squares, the counters must go diagonally to the left or right when they are moved. The counters can only move one square at a time and can only move forwards. However, once a counter reaches one of the four squares on the far side of the board, it becomes a king and is then allowed to move either forwards or backwards. So that you can recognize them quickly, the kings are usually crowned with a second counter and then move around the board as doubledeckers.

The object of the game of Draughts is *either* to capture all of your opponent's twelve counters *or* to block them in such a way that they cannot move. To capture an enemy counter all you have to do is jump over it.

Counters, of course, can only be moved on to squares that are empty, but to get to an empty square a counter can hop diagonally over another counter. If a player hops over one of his own counters he leaves the counter where it is. If he hops over an enemy counter, he captures it and takes it off the board. If a counter is in a position to jump over one of the enemy's counters it must do so, and it must go on jumping over all the enemy counters that it can, because by hopping over several counters in succession you can capture any number.

If you fail to capture an enemy's counter when you get the chance you are 'huffed'. That means that the enemy will *either* now take the counter (or the king) that failed to hop over an enemy counter when it could have done *or* will force you to take back your last move.

The first player to block his opponent or to capture all his counters is the winner.

GRASSHOPPER

Here's another game that calls for a chess board. You still need two players, but this time you can make do with ten counters each. It doesn't matter what they are – pebbles, coins, sugar lumps, postage stamps – so long as you can tell them apart.

The players place their counters in opposite corners of the board, on both the black and the white squares, in four diagonal rows, with one counter in the corner square, two in a line parallel with that, three in a line parallel with that and four in a final row parallel with that.

The aim of the game is to move all your counters from your corner across into your opponent's corner. He will be aiming to do exactly the same thing, of course, and the first one of you to make it is the winner.

You move your counters one square at a time and always on to empty squares. You can hop over other counters (your own or your opponent's) provided that you can land on an empty square immediately beyond the counter over which you have just hopped. And in any one move you can hop over any number of counters, providing that each time you can land on an empty square.

Toss to see who starts.

REVERSI

Reversi also calls for a chess board and two players. You need sixty-four counters which are black on one side and white on the other. Divide the counters equally between the two players and toss to see who begins.

The first player is Black and he starts by placing one of his thirty-two counters black-side up on one of the four central squares of the empty board. White then has to place his first piece on another of those four central squares. These four central squares are covered like this by the two players in the first four moves of the game.

The game continues with the two players taking it in turns to place one of their counters on any empty square that is adjacent to a square occupied by an enemy counter.

The aim of the game is to capture your enemy's counters and you can do this by trapping one of your enemy's counters between two of your own. For example, if Black puts a counter next to a White counter that already has a Black counter next to it, Black captures the White counter and turns it into a Black counter by turning it over. Any enemy counters that lie between a counter just played and another counter of the player's own colour, whether the line is diagonal, vertical or horizontal, are captured like this and they are always reversed to show the player's colour uppermost – hence, of course, the name of the game. The counters can change owners (and colours) many times in the course of a game.

The winner is the player who has the greatest number of counters with his colour showing after the sixty-fourth counter has been placed on the board.

String Games for a Rainy Day

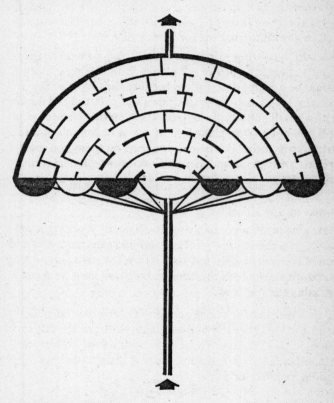

Umbrella Maze Number Three
[Solution on page 124]

STRING GAMES

The Eskimos, the American Indians and the head-hunters of New Guinea are all said to be people who have played with string for thousands of years. Nobody really knows who invented the first string game, nor where, nor how long ago. What is certain is that playing with string can be great fun and an absorbing pastime for a rainy day.

It is odd that string games are called string games because, strictly speaking, they're not *games* at all. 'String sculpture' would be a better description, because the object of the exercise is to make different shapes and patterns and figures with a small and simple loop of string. In this chapter you will find out how to make two of the most famous of all string 'sculptures', but before you start on them you must prepare your string and learn a few of the technical terms involved.

Preparing the string

How long is the piece of string you'll need? Working it out is easy: wrap the string eight times around your knuckles and you will have the right length. To turn the string into a loop you must tie the ends together and the best knot to use is probably the reef knot.

To tie a reef knot take one end of the string in your right hand and the other in your left hand. Now put the left over the right and take it under and then put the right over the left and take it under. Before you pull it tight the knot should look like this:

The technical terms

String games are more difficult to describe than they are to demonstrate and the technical terms that are used make it all seem much more complicated than it really is. However if you are going to learn any string games from books, you will have to get used to the technical terms and be sure to follow all the instructions thoroughly.

Each finger has a different name. They are called the thumb, index, middle, ring and little fingers. The index finger is next to the thumb, the middle finger is next to the index finger, the ring finger is next to the middle finger, and the little finger is next to the ring finger.

In making string figures the string will lie around your fingers in such a way that part of it will be nearer your body and part of it will be farther away. The part that is nearer is called 'the near string' and the part that is farther away is called 'the far string'.

If part of the string lies across the palm of the hand, that part is called 'the palmar string'.

In making the figures a finger may be passed either *over* or *under* a near string, a far string or a palmar string.

Points to remember

The normal position of the hands is with the palms facing inwards and the fingers pointing upwards. A return to this position is normal after each move.

When a loop is transferred from one finger to another, it must never be twisted. The original near string must still be on the near side and the original far string must still be on the far side.

The string should always be kept as near as possible to the tips of the fingers, but when a loop is picked up by a finger that already has a loop around it the new loop must obviously be kept above the original loop.

The instructions will seem complicated, but they do make sense and they will work if you follow them carefully. At first take each move quite slowly and read each instruction at least twice before you start.

A large number of string figures – including the two favourites described in this chapter – begin with one or other of two basic opening positions and to get you going it is a good idea to master these. They are called Position 1 and Opening A.

Position 1

1 Place the string over both little fingers and draw the hands apart.
2 With the thumbs pick up the near little finger strings from below and your hands should now look like this:

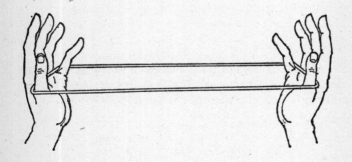

Opening A

1 Place the string on the hands in Position 1.
2 Put the right index finger under the left palmar string and draw it out as far as possible.
3 Put the left index finger under the right palmar string, in between the strings of the right index loop, and pick up the palmar string.
4 Draw the hands apart and you should find yourself in a situation that looks like this:

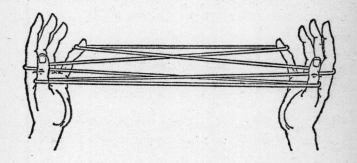

If you have got this far and not had too hard a time, you are a fast learner. Once you have mastered Position 1 and Opening A you are ready to make your first piece of authentic string sculpture. It's called a fish spear and if you think it doesn't really look like any fish spear you've ever seen, don't worry. None of the string figures seem to look very much like their names!

THE FISH SPEAR

1 Get into Position 1.
2 With the right index finger pick up from below the left palmar string and twist it down and away from you and then up towards you as you draw your hands apart.
3 With the left index finger pick up the right palmar string from below through the right index loop.
4 Release the right thumb and little finger and draw the string out tight. It should now look like this:

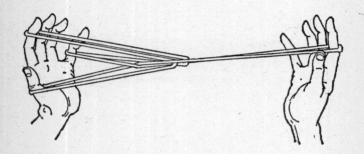

THE CANADIAN CANOE

1 Get into Opening A.
2 Pass the thumbs over the near index strings and pick up the far index strings from below.
3 Using your teeth lift off the thumbs their original near strings, but leave the loops you've just picked up on the thumbs.
4 Release the little fingers and pull the string tight. The result should look like this:

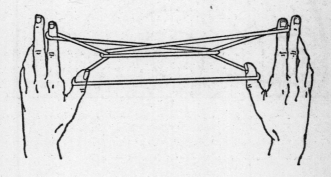

Puzzles for a Rainy Day

Umbrella Maze Number Four
[Solution on page 125]

CHALLENGE FOR A RAINY DAY

In this chapter you will find fifty puzzling brain-teasers. Some are old favourites, some are brand new. Some are simple, some are tough. You should be able to work out the answers to almost all of them in your head and none of the puzzles should take you more than five minutes to solve. Have a go at all of them and see how many you manage to get right (The answers are on pages 91–95). Give yourself 1 point for every correct answer and then see what rating your total gives you.

> 41–50 points: Congratulations – you're some kind of genius!
> 31–40 points: Brilliant!
> 21–30 points: Very good.
> 11–20 points: Average.
> 1–10 points: Poor.
> No points at all: Terrible!

NEXT PLEASE

What is the next letter in this series:

T, N, E, S, S, F, F, T, T, E, T, N, E, S, S—

THE ODD LETTER

Which letter doesn't belong in this series – and why?

A, E, F, H, I, K, L, M, N, O, T, V, W, X, Y, Z.

THE ODD NUMBER

Which number doesn't belong in this series – and why?

9, 27, 30, 15, 48, 7, 21, 33, 60, 90.

AGE-OLD PUZZLE

Hester is twice as old as Ben used to be when Hester happened to be as old as Ben is now. And Ben is now 18.

How old is Hester?

AGE AFTER AGE

Simon is twice as old as you were when Simon was your age. When you are as old as Simon is now, the sum of your ages will be 99.

How old is Simon? And how old are you?

AGES AND AGES

Grandpa Moses is 87½ years old. His wife, Grandma Moses, is only 50 years old. How many years ago was Grandpa Moses two and a quarter times as old as Grandma Moses?

WHAT AN AGE

When Mr Mulligan's age equals that of his father, he will be five times as old as his son is now. By then his son will be eight years older than Mr Mulligan is now. At the moment the combined ages of Mr Mulligan and his father total 100 years.

How old is Mr Mulligan's son?

WATER AND SQUASH

One tank is half full of water and the other tank is half full of orange squash. A spoonful of water is taken from the first tank and mixed with the orange squash in the second tank. A spoonful of the watered-down orange squash is now taken and mixed with the tank of water.

Is the amount of water taken from the first tank greater or less than the amount of orange squash taken from the second tank?

INTER-CITY

On the latest Inter-city express train, the journey from London to Edinburgh takes only four and a half hours and the journey back takes exactly the same time. Trains now leave each city every hour on the hour.

How many trains from Edinburgh will a passenger travelling from London to Edinburgh meet and pass on his journey?

THE UMBRELLA SALESMAN

Billy Brolly, the umbrella salesman, bought a number of handsome umbrellas for a total of £24. Sadly, taking them from the market to his shop, he lost two of them. He sold the rest for a total of £25.20 and managed to make a profit of 20p. on each umbrella.

How many umbrellas did he originally buy?

VERSE

A noun there is of plural number,
A foe to ease and peaceful slumber.
Now any other noun you take
By adding 's' you plural make,
But if you add an 's' to this
Strange is the metamorphosis:
Plural is plural now no more,
And sweet what bitter was before!

So what is the word the verse is all about? To give you a
clue, it contains five letters.

WORSE VERSE

There are three words missing in this short poem. Each word
contains the same six letters, but in a different order. Can
you find the missing words?

Through the —— trees
Softly coo the doves,
Let a —— breeze
—— youthful loves.

WORST VERSE

And in this couplet the three missing words each contain the
same seven letters in a different order. What are they?

He —— to be —— as a wonderful shot.
He potted a dog and —— was his lot!

NOT SO FAST

A man makes a trip in his car and on the outward journey travels at an average speed of 30 m.p.h. On the return journey he averages a speed of 20 m.p.h. what is his average speed for the journey as a whole?

THE SNAIL ON THE WALL

A snail climbs up a wall which is twenty metres high at the rate of three metres each day, but poor creature, he slips back two metres every night. Now long will it take him to get to the top?

THE FIGG FAMILY

Mr and Mrs Ferdinand Figg had a happy family of sons and daughters. Each daughter had an equal number of brothers and sisters, but each son had twice as many sisters as brothers.

How many boys and girls were there in the family?

THE BLIND BEGGAR

The poor, blind beggar had a brother who died. The man who died, however, had no brother. So what relation was the poor, blind beggar to the man who died?

THE FUNN FAMILY

In 1964 Mr Freddie Funn's age added to that of his wife, Mrs Flossie Funn, was exactly ten times the sum of the ages of all their children. By 1966 it was only six times the sum, and by 1972 it had fallen to three times the sum.

How many children are there in the Funn family?

HOW FAR?

Cyril Sweet was due to meet Suzie Sour at Leicester Town Hall at two o'clock. If he left home on his bicycle and raced to Leicester at 15 m.p.h. he would arrive at one o'clock, and if he travelled at 10 m.p.h. he would arrive at three o'clock.

How far did Cyril Sweet live from Leicester Town Hall?

THE FOUR GREEDY GIRLS

Four greedy girls were given a large tin of toffees. They counted out the toffees and found there were 233! Then they grabbed them. Mary was the greediest and managed to get 20 more toffees than Jane, 53 more than Kate and 71 more than Elizabeth.

One more thing you ought to know: because they were all greedy they even fought over one of the toffees and divided it between them. So how many toffees did each girl get?

BIRDS OF A FEATHER

A rich man goes into a pet shop and buys twenty birds for £20.00. The parrots cost £4.00 each, the minah birds cost 50p each and the canaries cost 25p each.

How many parrots, minah birds and canaries did the rich man buy?

THE OLD MAN

I asked the old man how old he was and he replied, 'To tell you the truth, lad, I don't rightly remember. I do know that I went to school when I was four-and-a-half years old and that I stayed at school for a sixth of my life. I know I was in the army for a fifth of my life. And when I left the army I spent a quarter of my life as a road-sweeper. I've now spent a third of my life in retirement. So you tell me, how old am I?'

Well, how old is he?

FATHER AND DAUGHTER

Mr Sam Smith's age added to that of his daughter, Miss Sally Smith, comes to exactly 100 years. Mr Smith's age multiplied by three and divided by seven gives a figure which is equal to his daughter's age.

How old is Sam and how old is Sally?

THE FLY AND THE BOYS ON THE BICYCLE

Two boys, twenty miles apart, set off on their bicycles at exactly the same moment and travelled towards each other along a straight and empty road. They were both riding at 10 m.p.h. At the same moment as the boys set off, a fly perched on the nose of one of the boys set off and flew at 15 m.p.h. towards the other rider. When it reached him it touched down on his nose and then set off again flying back to the first rider. It kept this up, flying from one boy's nose to the other, until finally the two boys met and the poor fly collapsed from exhaustion.

How many miles did the fly travel before it finally collapsed?

ESCAPE!

A prisoner escaped from Dartmoor Prison and had a half-hour start on the two prison officers and the bloodhound who were sent to catch him. The prisoner was running at three miles an hour, while the prison officers were running at four miles an hour and the bloodhound was tearing along at twelve miles an hour. Every time the dog reached the prisoner he ran back to the prison officers, then back to the prisoner, then back to the prison officers, and he kept running back and forth like this until eventually the prison officers caught their man.

How many miles did the dog travel before the prisoner was caught?

MIKE AND JOHN

The combined ages of Mike and John are 44 years. Mike is twice as old as John was when Mike was half as old as John will be when John is three times as old as Mike was when Mike was three times as old as John.

How old is Mike? How old is John?

THE PICTURE ON THE WALL

Pointing to the picture of a man that was hanging on the wall, Miss Jezebel Jones said to her father, 'That man's mother was my mother's mother-in-law.'

How was Miss Jones related to the man in the picture?

THE MARRIAGE OF BERTIE BROWN

In the summer of 1889 Mr Bertie Brown married the sister of his widow. How did he come to do that?

CLASSIC PUNCTUATION

Here is one of the best-known puzzles in the world. Try to punctuate this famous sentence: 'Tom where Dick had had had had had had had had had had the examiner's approval.'

A WEEK TO REMEMBER

When the day after tomorrow is yesterday, today will be as far away from Sunday as today was from Sunday when the day before yesterday was tomorrow.

What day is it?

A WORD TO REMEMBER

Can *you* think of an English word that contains twenty-eight letters?

CAT COUNT

A hexagonal room had a cat in each corner, five cats before each cat and a cat on every cat's tail.

How many cats were there in the room?

ANOTHER PICTURE ON THE WALL

Pointing to another picture of a different man, Mrs Joyce Jones remarked:

'I've no sister or brother, you may think me wild,
'But that man's mother was my mother's child!'

How was Mrs Jones related to the man in the picture?

THE BRICK TRICK

If a brick weighs 9 kilos and half a brick, what is the weight of a brick and a half?

JACK AND JILL

Jack is 24 years old. Jack is twice as old as Jill was when Jack was as old as Jill is now.

How old is Jill?

ALPHABETICAL SENTENCE

'A quick brown fox jumps over the lazy dog' is a nine-word sentence that contains every single letter of the alphabet. Can you think of an eight-word sentence that also manages to include all twenty-six letters of the alphabet?

THE TWO CLOCKS

If one clock takes eight seconds to strike eight o'clock, how many seconds will it take to strike twelve o'clock?
If another clock takes six seconds to strike six o'clock, how many seconds will it take to strike twelve o'clock?

A WELL-KNOWN PROVERB

Add just one letter of the alphabet to this group of letters and turn them into a well-known proverb:

EEBRAWLKNNWOROPL

THE FOUR EXPLORERS

Four bold explorers made a journey into the Sahara desert.
Each explorer carried enough food to last him for five full
days. After the party had been out for one day, one of the
explorers decided to turn back, and he took with him just
enough food to last until he got back to the starting point. A
day later a second explorer did the same thing. And on the
next day so did a third.

How many days' journey was the last explorer able to make
into the desert and still be able to return safely?

TWO MEN IN MONTE CARLO

Bill and Ben were on holiday in Monte Carlo. One day they
decided to visit the casino and enjoy a little gambling. When
they went in Bill had £8 for every £5 Ben had. By the time
they left the casino each of them had won £9, and Bill now
had £11 for every £8 Ben had.

How much money did each of them start with?

CLOCK FACE

At what time between three o'clock and four o'clock will
the hands on a clock face be in a straight line?

POST OFFICE PUZZLE

In the Post Office's central sorting depot for Hampshire an envelope appeared with this written on it:

Wood
John
Hants

Who was the letter addressed to and in what town did he live?

ONE MAN AND HIS DOG

With just three straight strokes of your pencil, draw a picture of a man carrying a walking stick under his arm accompanied by his dog walking past a building.

THE MISSING LETTER

What's the missing letter in this series – and why?

YADYNIARAROFSEMAGDNANUFFOKOOBTH-INK

A PAGE WITHOUT PUNCTUATION

Can you supply the correct punctuation for the strange sentences that follow?

1. he said that that that that that woman said ought to have been which
2. it was and I said not but
3. the murderer spoke angrily half an hour after he was hanged
4. time flies you cannot they pass by at such irregular intervals
5. Esau Wood saw a saw saw wood as no other wood saw Wood saw would saw wood of all the wood saws Wood ever saw saw wood Wood never saw a wood saw that would saw wood as the wood saw Wood saw saw wood would saw wood and I never saw a wood saw that would saw wood as the wood saw Wood saw would saw until I saw Wood saw wood with the wood saw Esau Wood saw saw wood

ANSWERS TO THE PUZZLES FOR A RAINY DAY

NEXT PLEASE
F. The letters are the initials of the numbers 20 to 5 starting at 20 and going down to 5.

THE ODD LETTER
O. All the other letters are made up of straight lines when written as capitals.

THE ODD NUMBER
7. It's the only number in the series that cannot be divided by 3.

AGE-OLD PUZZLE
24

AGE AFTER AGE
You are 33 and Simon is 44.

AGES AND AGES
Twenty years ago.

WHAT AN AGE
13.

WATER AND SQUASH
The same.

INTER-CITY
Nine trains.

THE UMBRELLA SALESMAN
Twenty.

VERSE
Cares. (When you add an 's' it becomes caress!)

WORSE VERSE
Through the FOREST trees
Softy coo the doves,
Let a SOFTER breeze
FOSTER youthful loves.

WORST VERSE
He ASPIRED to be PRAISED as a wonderful shot.
He potted a dog and DESPAIR was his lot!

NOT SO FAST
24 m.p.h. Supposing the outward journey had been 60 miles, it would have taken the man two hours. The return journey would also have been 60 miles, but it would have taken the man three hours, which means that the man would have taken a total of five hours to travel 120 miles. Divide 120 by 5 and you will find that the man's overall average speed was 24 m.p.h.

THE SNAIL ON THE WALL
Eighteen days. In seventeen days the snail manages to climb seventeen metres. On the eighteenth day he climbs three metres as usual and on that day manages to get out because he has reached twenty metres without slipping back.

THE FIGG FAMILY
Three boys and four girls.

THE BLIND BEGGAR
The poor blind beggar was the *sister* of the man who died.

THE FUNN FAMILY
Three children.

HOW FAR?
60 miles.

THE FOUR GREEDY GIRLS
Mary took 94¼; Jane took 74¼; Kate took 41¼; Elizabeth took 23¼.

BIRDS OF A FEATHER
He bought three parrots, fifteen minah birds and two canaries.

THE OLD MAN
Ninety years old.

FATHER AND DAUGHTER
Sam is 70 years old; Sally is 30 years old.

THE FLY AND THE BOYS ON THE BICYCLES
15 miles.

ESCAPE!
18 miles.

MIKE AND JOHN
Mike is 27½; John is 16½.

THE PICTURE ON THE WALL
She was his daughter.

THE MARRIAGE OF BERTIE BROWN
He married the sister first. It was later that he married the woman who became his widow

CLASSIC PUNCTUATION
'Tom, where Dick had had 'had had' had had 'had'. 'Had had' had had the examiner's approval.'

A WEEK TO REMEMBER
Sunday.

A WORD TO REMEMBER
Antidisestablishmentarianism!

CAT COUNT
Six cats.

ANOTHER PICTURE ON THE WALL
She was his mother.

THE BRICK TRICK
27 kilos.

JACK AND JILL
Jill is 24.

ALPHABETICAL SENTENCE
Pack my box with five dozen liquor jugs.

THE TWO CLOCKS
12⁴⁄₇ seconds; 13⅛ seconds.

A WELL-KNOWN PROVERB
Add a V to the letters, unjumble them and you can make the phrase 'A WELL-KNOWN PROVERB'!

THE FOUR EXPLORERS
Four days out and four days back.

TWO MEN IN MONTE CARLO
Bill had £24 and Ben had £15.

CLOCK FACE
At 3.49.

POST OFFICE PUZZLE
John Underwood in Andover – because on the envelopes
'John' was under 'Wood' and over 'Hants'!

ONE MAN AND HIS DOG
The man has disappeared
behind the building, so all
you can see is the wall and
his walking stick and the
dog's tail going behind it.

THE MISSING LETTER
G. All together the letters spell KNIGHT BOOK OF FUN
AND GAMES FOR A RAINY DAY backwards!

A PAGE WITHOUT PUNCTUATION
1 He said that that 'that' that that woman said, ought to
   have been 'which'.
2 It was 'and' I said, not 'but'.
3 The murderer spoke angrily. Half an hour after he was
   hanged.
4 Time flies? You cannot! They pass by at such irregular
   intervals.
5 Esau Wood saw a saw saw wood as no other wood-saw
   Wood saw would saw wood. Of all the wood-saws Wood
   ever saw saw wood, Wood never saw a wood-saw that
   would saw wood as the wood-saw Wood saw saw wood
   would saw wood, and I never saw a wood-saw that
   would saw wood as the wood-saw Wood saw would saw,
   until I saw Wood saw wood with the wood-saw Esau
   Wood saw saw wood.

Quizzes for a Rainy Day

Umbrella Maze Number Five
[Solution on page 126]

THE RAINY DAY QUIZ

1 In the film *Singin' in the Rain* who sang the title song?
  (a) Frank Sinatra.
  (b) Fred Astaire.
  (c) Gene Kelly.
  (d) Bing Crosby.

2 Where will you find the world's rainiest spot?
  (a) In India.
  (b) In Japan.
  (c) In Ceylon.
  (d) In Nigeria.

3 In the musical *My Fair Lady* there is a song about the rain and where it falls. Is it:
  (a) In a park in Denmark?
  (b) On a highland in Iceland?
  (c) On a plain in Spain?
  (d) On a hilly in Chile?

4 Who was it who stepped in a puddle on a visit to Gloucester?
  (a) Dr Kildare.
  (b) Dr Foster.
  (c) Dr Dolittle.
  (d) Dr Muddle.

5 What is the name of Prince Rainier's wife? She was once a famous film star.
  (a) Grace Darling.
  (b) Gracie Fields.
  (c) Grace Grossmith.
  (d) Grace Kelly.

(Answers on page 116)

ALL ABOUT WOMEN QUIZ

1 Who was the first woman to take her seat as a Member of Parliament?
    (a) Marie Lloyd.
    (b) Emily Pankhurst.
    (c) Glencora Palliser.
    (d) Nancy Astor.

2 For what was Dame Margaret Rutherford best known? Was she:
    (a) The first woman in space?
    (b) A scientist?
    (c) An actress?
    (d) The first woman to run a four-minute mile?

3 Who was Henry VIII's first wife?
    (a) Katharine of Aragon.
    (b) Katherine of Russia.
    (c) Katherine Boyle.
    (d) Catherine Parr.

4 For what was Nellie Melba best known?
    (a) Her brilliant ballet dancing.
    (b) Her beautiful singing.
    (c) Her wonderful writing.
    (d) Her burnt toast.

5 In 1930 a lady called Amy Johnson did something extraordinary. Did she:
    (a) Swim from Dover to Calais?
    (b) Walk across the Niagara Falls on a tightrope?
    (c) Fly from Europe to Africa?
    (d) Make a solo flight to Australia?

(Answers on page 116)

ALL ABOUT MEN QUIZ

1 Who was Britain's youngest Prime Minister?
   (a) William Gladstone.
   (b) Anthony Eden.
   (c) Alec Douglas-Home.
   (d) William Pitt the Younger.

2 For what was Sir Donald Wolfit best known? Was he:
   (a) A scientist?
   (b) An explorer?
   (c) A murderer?
   (d) An actor?

3 Who was Queen Victoria's husband?
   (a) Prince Charles.
   (b) Prince Albert.
   (c) Prince Edward.
   (d) Prince George.

4 For what was Enrico Caruso best known?
   (a) His brilliant cooking.
   (b) His beautiful singing.
   (c) His wonderful writing.
   (d) His Caribbean cruises.

5 In 1926 a man called John Logie Baird did something
   extraordinary. Did he:
   (a) Invent television?
   (b) Fly the Atlantic?
   (c) Discover penicillin?
   (d) Make an expedition to the North Pole?

(Answers on page 116)

SPORTING QUIZ

1 With which sport do you associate the terms 'bag', 'battery', 'block', 'bunt' and 'base hit'?
   (a) Baseball.   (c) Table tennis.
   (b) Basketball.   (d) Hurdling.

2 In which game are some of the chief shots known as 'the trail', 'the draw', 'the tap', 'the guard', 'the rest' and 'the yard one'?
   (a) Cricket.   (c) Bowls.
   (b) Snooker.   (d) Tennis.

3 In which sport are there positions known as 'gully', 'slips', 'point' and 'silly point'?
   (a) Lacrosse.   (c) Rugger.
   (b) Hockey.   (d) Cricket.

4 If somebody carrying a mallet warned you, 'I may try to triple-peel your Blue and peg it out,' what game would be involved?
   (a) Ice Hockey.   (c) Polo.
   (b) Croquet.   (d) Golf.

5 With what sport are the phrases 'free kick', 'knock on', 'punt' and 'loose scrum' associated?
   (a) Rowing.   (c) Rugger.
   (b) Netball.   (d) Soccer.

(Answers on page 116)

CAPITAL QUIZ

1 Is the capital of Ethiopia
    (a) Addis Ababa?
    (b) Libreville?
    (c) Accra?
    (d) Nairobi?

2 Is the capital of Hungary
    (a) Reykjavik?
    (b) Athens?
    (c) Oslo?
    (d) Budapest?

3 Is the capital of New Zealand
    (a) Canberra?
    (b) Brisbane?
    (c) Wellington?
    (d) Hobart?

4 Is the capital of Argentina
    (a) La Paz?
    (b) Buenos Aires?
    (c) Bogota?
    (d) Lima?

5 Is the capital of Burma
    (a) Tokyo?
    (b) Rangoon?
    (c) Dacca?
    (d) Beirut?

6 Is the capital of Cuba
   (a) Toronto?
   (b) Kingston?
   (c) Havana?
   (d) Port au Prince?

7 Is the capital of Switzerland
   (a) Zurich?
   (b) Bonn?
   (c) Geneva?
   (d) Berne?

8 Is the capital of Venezuela
   (a) Santiago?
   (b) Caracas?
   (c) Brasilia?
   (d) Montevideo?

9 Is the capital of Egypt
   (a) Cairo?
   (b) Tehran?
   (c) Baghdad?
   (d) Amman?

10 Is the capital of Nigeria
   (a) Lagos?
   (b) Niamey?
   (c) Dakar?
   (d) Cape Town?

(Answers on page 117)

THE HIGHEST AND LOWEST QUIZ

1 The tallest building in Europe is 985 feet high. Is it:
    (a) The Post Office Tower?
    (b) The Leaning Tower of Pisa?
    (c) The Eiffel Tower?
    (d) Canterbury Cathedral?

2 How deep is the deepest ocean? The answer is at least 36,000 feet at its deepest. Is that ocean:
    (a) The Atlantic?
    (b) The Arctic?
    (c) The Indian?
    (d) The Pacific?

3 What is England's highest point?
    (a) Ben Nevis.
    (b) Snowdon.
    (c) Scafell Pike.
    (d) Carrantuohill.

4 The world's tallest man was an American called Robert Pershing Wadlow. He was born in 1918 and died in 1940. How tall do you think he was?
    (a) 6 feet 11 inches.
    (b) 7 feet 11 inches.
    (c) 8 feet 11 inches.
    (d) 9 feet 11 inches.

5 The world's deepest sea goes down to 23,000 feet. Is it:
    (a) The Caribbean?
    (b) The Mediterranean?
    (c) The North Sea?
    (d) The Red Sea?

(Answers on page 117)

CURRENCY QUIZ

1 In which country would you find a coin called a
   RAND?
      (a) Uganda.
      (b) South Africa.
      (c) France.
      (d) Belgium.

2 In which country would you find a RUPEE?
      (a) Germany.
      (b) Australia.
      (c) Bolivia.
      (d) Pakistan.

3 In which country would you find a DRACHMA?
      (a) Poland.
      (b) Canada.
      (c) Greece.
      (d) India.

4 In which country would you find a MARK?
      (a) Eire.
      (b) Burma.
      (c) Germany.
      (d) Finland.

5 In which country would you find a DOLLAR?
      (a) Yugoslavia.
      (b) Barbados.
      (c) The Netherlands.
      (d) United States of America.

(Answers on page 117)

DICTIONARY QUIZ

1 Is a DROMEDARY
  (a) A South American lizard?
  (b) A Greek coin?
  (c) An Arabian Camel?
  (d) An Arabian Knight?

2 Is a HAMLET
  (a) A small piece of bacon?
  (b) A small Danish prince?
  (c) A small piece of jewellery?
  (d) A small village?

3 Is a JAMB
  (a) Part of a door?
  (b) Part of a fruit?
  (c) Part of a sandwich?
  (d) Part of a musical instrument?

4 Is a PHILANTHROPIST
  (a) Someone who loves mankind?
  (b) Someone who hates English people?
  (c) Someone who collects butterflies?
  (d) Someone who is a philosopher?

5 Is an APIARY
  (a) A place where monkeys are kept?
  (b) A place where bees are kept?
  (c) A place where birds are kept?
  (d) A place where pigs are kept?

6 Is a CONFABULATION
   (a) A kind of conversation?
   (b) A kind of pudding?
   (c) A kind of wild animal?
   (d) A kind of wild flower?

7 Is a FUCHSIA
   (a) A dog?
   (b) A plant?
   (c) A poison?
   (d) A fish?

8 Is a SALOPIAN
   (a) Someone from Salisbury?
   (b) Someone from Shropshire?
   (c) Someone from Pompeii?
   (d) Someone from Salop?

9 Is a TRAPPIST
   (a) A kind of hunter?
   (b) A kind of doctor?
   (c) A kind of savage?
   (d) A kind of monk?

10 Is a GROG
   (a) A drink?
   (b) An old man?
   (c) A ship?
   (d) A worm?

11 Is a LEASH
    (a) A bird's beak?
    (b) A cat's basket?
    (c) A horse's hoof?
    (d) A dog's lead?

12 Is a PENTATHLON
    (a) A Greek temple?
    (b) A serious illness?
    (c) An athletic competition?
    (d) A seaside resort?

13 Is a PRIVET
    (a) A lavatory?
    (b) A hedge?
    (d) A soldier?
    (d) A priest?

14 Is a RISOTTO
    (a) Something to plant in the garden?
    (b) Something to wash clothes with?
    (c) Something to eat?
    (d) Something to sit on?

15 Is a SAGE
    (a) A rice pudding?
    (b) A wise man?
    (c) A herb?
    (d) An umbrella?

16 Is a CHAMELEON
    (a) A comedian?
    (b) A deer?
    (c) A leather mop?
    (d) A lizard?

17 Is a CLOG
    (a) A kind of simpleton?
    (b) A kind of shoe?
    (c) A kind of vegetable?
    (d) A kind of Christmas decoration?

18 Is an EPAULETTE
    (a) Part of a uniform?
    (b) Part of a car?
    (c) Part of a pyramid?
    (d) Part of the human body?

19 Is a GUFFAW
    (a) A precipice?
    (b) An Indian chief?
    (c) A mythical creature?
    (d) A laugh?

20 Is a BILL
    (a) A bird's beak?
    (b) A demand for money?
    (c) An old weapon?
    (d) A kind of poster?

(Answers on page 118)

TOP TEN QUIZ

In the column on the left you will find a list of the populations of the ten largest cities in the world. In the column on the right you'll find the names of those ten cities – but the list isn't in the right order. Can you put it in order?

1	11,571,899	PEKING
2	11,403,744	LONDON
3	10,820,000	CHICAGO
4	8,352,900	MOSCOW
5	8,000,000	NEW YORK
6	7,570,000	MEXICO CITY
7	7,379,014	LOS ANGELES
8	7,172,000	TOKYO
9	7,032,075	SHANGHAI
10	6,978,947	BUENOS AIRES

(Answers on page 118)

WONDERS OF THE ANCIENT WORLD QUIZ

Here are the names of four of the Seven Wonders of the Ancient World:

THE TOMB OF MAUSOLUS AT HALICARNASSUS
THE TEMPLE OF DIANA AT EPHESUS
THE STATUE OF JUPITER, OLYMPUS
THE PHAROS OF ALEXANDRIA

Can you name the other three?

(Answers on page 119)

WHAT-DO-YOU-KNOW QUIZ

1 Which is the world's longest river?
   (a) The Amazon.
   (b) The Nile.
   (c) The Yangtze.
   (d) The Mississippi.

2 Britain's longest railway tunnel stretches for 4 miles and 628 yards. Where would you find it?
   (a) Disley.
   (b) Sevenoaks.
   (c) Totley.
   (d) Severn.

3 Who was the first President of France's Fifth Republic?
   (a) The Emperor Napoleon.
   (b) Marshal Pétain.
   (c) General de Gaulle.
   (d) Georges Pompidou.

4 There has only ever been one English Pope. He became Pope in 1154. What was his name? Was it:
   (a) Pope John XXIII?
   (b) Pope Leo XIII?
   (c) Pope Benedict II?
   (d) Pope Adrian IV?

5 There are five Cinque Ports. Hastings, New Romney, Hythe and Dover are four of them. What is the fifth?
   (a) Portsmouth.
   (b) Ramsgate.
   (c) Plymouth.
   (d) Sandwich.

6 Tarzan had a girlfriend. What was her name?
   (a) Florence.
   (b) Jane.
   (c) Cinderella.
   (d) Olive Oyl.

7 Who designed St Paul's Cathedral?
   (a) Sir Basil Spence.
   (b) Sir Isaac Newton.
   (c) Sir Christopher Wren.
   (d) Sir Walter Raleigh.

8 Who was the first English printer?
   (a) William Tell.
   (b) Ben Jonson.
   (c) William Caxton.
   (d) Samuel Johnson.

9 Arthur Conan Doyle was the creator of which famous detective?
   (a) Hercule Poirot.
   (b) Maigret.
   (c) Fabian of the Yard.
   (d) Sherlock Holmes.

10 Of these four English poets, which has been Poet Laureate?
   (a) John Dryden.
   (b) John Betjeman.
   (c) John Masefield.
   (d) William Wordsworth.

11 Who was the British Prime Minister at the beginning of the second World War?
   (a) Winston Churchill.
   (b) Clement Attlee.
   (c) Neville Chamberlain.
   (d) Lloyd George.

12 How is John Osborne well known? Is he:
   (a) A biscuit manufacturer?
   (b) A spaceman?
   (c) A playwright?
   (d) A musician?

13 How many pounds are there in 1 kilo?
   (a) 1.105 lbs.
   (b) 2.205 lbs.
   (c) 5.505 lbs.
   (d) 6.605 lbs.

14 What is the name of Princess Alexandra's husband?
   (a) Mark Phillips.
   (b) Mark Carlisle.
   (c) Angus Robertson.
   (d) Angus Ogilvy.

15 Who wrote the play *All's Well that Ends Well*?
   (a) Noel Coward.
   (b) William Shakespeare.
   (c) Arthur Miller.
   (d) Frankie Howerd.

(Answers on page 119)

TRUE OR FALSE QUIZ

1 Charles Dickens wrote *Pride and Prejudice*. True or false?

2 Oslo is the capital of Norway. True or false?

3 The volcano Mount Etna in Sicily is extinct. True or false?

4 Kilimanjaro is Africa's highest mountain. True or false?

5 The Vatican City has a population of 1,000. True or false?

6 President Kennedy was assassinated in Houston, Texas, in 1963. True or false?

7 Neil Armstrong was the first American in space. True or false?

8 Jane Austen wrote *A Tale of Two Cities*. True or false?

9 Abraham Lincoln was the first President of the United States of America. True or false?

10 The sinking of the S.S. *Titanic* was in 1912. True or false?

11 The U.S.S.R. stands for the Union of Socialist Soviet Revolutionaries. True or false?

12 Alexander Graham Bell invented the telephone. True or false?

13 Julie Andrews starred in the film of the musical *My Fair Lady*. True or false?

14 Adolf Hitler became Chancellor of Germany in 1933. True or false?

15 Queen Victoria was nicknamed the Virgin Queen. True or false?

16 England won the World Cup in 1970. True or false?

17 Elvis Presley is an American singer who was born in 1935. True or false?

18 Gerald R. Ford became the thirty-seventh President of the United States of America. True or false?

19 Tom and Jerry are cartoon characters invented by Walt Disney. True or false?

20 Greenland is the world's largest island. True or false?

21 King Kong is the ruler of the African kingdom of the Congo. True or false?

22 Mrs Doasyouwouldbedoneby is a character in *The Water Babies* by Kingsley Amis. True or false?

23 Ottawa is the capital of Canada. True or false?

24 The world's oldest university is Oxford University. True or false?

25 Henry VI was England's youngest monarch and came to the throne when he was less than nine months old. True or false?

26 The ylang-ylang is a kind of tree to be found in Malaya. True or false?

27 Dr Barnado wrote a famous book about how to bring up children, called *Baby and Child Care*. True or false?

28 The actress Elizabeth Taylor has been married five times. Her husbands include Sir Charles Forte, Mike Todd, Bobby Fischer and Richard Burton. True or false?

29 Edmund Hillary reached the summit of Mount Everest in 1953. True or false?

30 The Mona Lisa is a famous painting by Vincent Van Gogh. True or false?

31 The London Underground was opened in 1890. True or false?

32 Compulsory National Service ended in Great Britain in 1960. True or false?

33 Rin Tin Tin, Lassie and Dougal are all the names of dogs made famous in the cinema or on television. True or false?

34 *Around the World in Eighty Days* is the title of a novel by Jules Verne. True or false?

35 The Beatles and the Monkees are the names of two species of wild life. True or false?

36 In 1960 Princess Margaret married Anthony Armslength Jones. True or false?

37 *The News of the World* is the world's best-selling newspaper. True or false?

38 The Isle of Wight is separated from the coast of Hampshire by the Solent. True or false?

39 Peter Pan was looked after by a tiny fairy called Wendy. True or false?

40 Mohammed Ali is the name of a Buddhist prophet. True or false?

(Answers on page 120)

ANSWERS TO THE QUIZZES FOR RAINY DAY

RAINY DAY QUIZ
1 (c)
2 (a)
3 (c)
4 (b)
5 (d)

ALL ABOUT WOMEN QUIZ
1 (d)
2 (c)
3 (a)
4 (b)
5 (d)

ALL ABOUT MEN QUIZ
1 (d)
2 (d)
3 (b)
4 (b)
5 (a)

SPORTING QUIZ
1 (a)
2 (c)
3 (d)
4 (b)
5 (c)

CAPITAL QUIZ

1 (a)
2 (d)
3 (c)
4 (b)
5 (b)
6 (c)
7 (d)
8 (b)
9 (a)
10 (a)

THE HIGHEST AND LOWEST QUIZ

1 (c)
2 (d)
3 (c) (Ben Nevis is in Scotland, Snowdon is in Wales and Carrantuohill is in Ireland.)
4 (c)
5 (a)

CURRENCY QUIZ

1 (b)
2 (d)
3 (c)
4 (c)
5 (d)

DICTIONARY QUIZ

1 (c)
2 (d)
3 (a)
4 (a)
5 (b)
6 (a)
7 (b)
8 (b)
9 (d)
10 (a)
11 (d)
12 (c)
13 (b)
14 (c)
15 (b) *and* (c)
16 (d)
17 (b)
18 (a)
19 (d)
20 *All four!*

TOP TEN QUIZ

1 NEW YORK, U.S.A.
2 TOKYO, Japan.
3 SHANGHAI, China.
4 BUENOS AIRES, Argentina.
5 MEXICO CITY, Mexico.
6 PEKING, China.
7 LONDON, England.
8 MOSCOW, U.S.S.R.
9 LOS ANGELES, U.S.A.
10 CHICAGO, U.S.A.

WONDERS OF THE ANCIENT WORLD QUIZ
The remaining three of the Seven Wonders of the Ancient
World are:

    THE PYRAMIDS OF EGYPT
    THE HANGING GARDENS OF BABYLON
    THE COLOSSUS OF RHODES

WHAT-DO-YOU-KNOW QUIZ
  1 (b)
  2 (d)
  3 (c)
  4 (d)
  5 (d)
  6 (b)
  7 (c)
  8 (c)
  9 (d)
10 *They all have*
11 (c)
12 (c)
13 (b)
14 (d)
15 (b)

TRUE OR FALSE QUIZ

1 False. Jane Austen wrote *Pride and Prejudice*.
2 True.
3 False.
4 True.
5 True.
6 False. President Kennedy was assassinated in Dallas, Texas.
7 False. Neil Armstrong was the first man to set foot on the moon.
8 False. Charles Dickens wrote *A Tale of Two Cities*.
9 False. George Washington was the first President of the United States of America.
10 True.
11 False. The U.S.S.R. stands for the Union of Soviet Socialist Republics.
12 True.
13 False. Julie Andrews starred in *My Fair Lady* on the stage. In the film the part was played by Audrey Hepburn.
14 True.
15 False. It was Queen Elizabeth I who was nicknamed the Virgin Queen.
16 False. England won the World Cup in 1966.
17 True.
18 True.
19 False. Tom and Jerry were created by Fred Quimby.
20 True. Greenland is the world's largest island excluding Australia, which does not really count as it is also a continent.
21 False. King Kong was a giant gorilla first made famous in a film called *King Kong* in 1932.
22 False. *The Water Babies* is by Charles Kingsley.

23 True

24 False. The University of Karueein at Fez in Morocco is the world's oldest. It was founded in 859. Oxford is England's oldest University and came into being around 1167.

25 True.

26 True.

27 False. Dr Benjamin Spock is the author of the famous book on child care.

28 False. Elizabeth Taylor's five husbands have been Conrad Hilton Jr, Michael Wilding, Mike Todd, Eddie Fisher and Richard Burton.

29 True.

30 False. The Mona Lisa is by Leonardo da Vinci.

31 True.

32 True.

33 True.

34 True.

35 False. The Beatles and the Monkees are the names of two pop groups, now disbanded.

36 False. In 1960 Princess Margaret married Anthony Armstrong-Jones, now Lord Snowdon.

37 True.

38 True.

39 False. Tinkerbell was the name of Peter Pan's fairy.

40 False. Mohammed Ali, formerly Cassius Clay, is a boxer.

Umbrella Maze Number One

Umbrella Maze Number Two

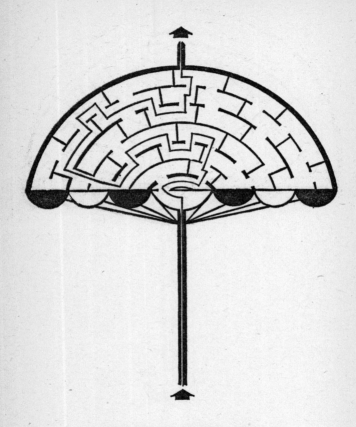

Umbrella Maze Number Three